Practical Sales Ideas For Small Business

Proven Techniques To Close More Deals And Delight Your Customers

Steven Imke

Produced in the United States of America

First Printing, 2016

ISBN-13: 978-1534702172
ISBN-10: 1534702172

KSI Enterprises
395 Scrub Oak Circle
Monument CO 80132

www.SteveBizBlog.com

About the Author

Steve's first foray into the world of small business came when he was an Invisible Fencing dealer. He operated this business on a part-time basis while remaining employed by a Fortune 500 company called Digital Equipment Corporation (DEC). While the Invisible Fencing business was not very successful for Steve, it was a valuable opportunity for him to learn important lessons about business in a relatively low-risk environment.

After ending his relationship with Invisible Fencing, he worked on a business plan for a new business idea and waited for the right opportunity to present itself. In 1994, DEC fell on hard times. Instead of bemoaning this turbulent economic tide, Steve capitalized on this opportunity. He quit his day job at DEC to found Horizon Interactive, a documentation and training company. In fact, Horizon Interactive became a vendor for DEC.

Over the next few years, Steve and his partners executed the business plan. The business grew to over $3 million in annual sales and opened offices in several states. Horizon Interactive's success drew the attention of Interleaf, a publicly held company out of Massachusetts. In 1999, Interleaf acquired Horizon Interactive.

As part of the acquisition, Steve was offered the position of VP of Operations for their services division. Under his leadership, Interleaf acquired two more businesses like

Horizon Interactive. The company grew the services side of the business from a combined $8 million in revenue to over $32 million in sales during the next two years.

In 2001, Interleaf was acquired by Broadvision, a California company during the height of the dot com era. Broadvision primarily acquired Interleaf for their XML engineers who worked on the product side of the business. Needing to divest himself from the services business, Steve and a former business partner acquired the assets of Interleaf's service business and started IC Interactive. They operated the business for a few more years until they sold it in 2003.

Being a serial entrepreneur, Steve has started and still operates three different businesses. One of his businesses is focused on real estate. The second one is focused on oil and gas. His third business is a company designed to help high net-worth investors understand the ins and outs of investing in oil and gas direct participation programs.

Steve has volunteered his time since 2003 as a mentor for SCORE, a local organization dedicated to helping entrepreneurs. He has acted as their Chapter Chairman for several years. He is also an advisory board member of his local Small Business Development Center (SBDC). In additions to his advisory role, he also acts as a counselor for the SBDC since 2003. In 2012, Steve acted as the interim director of SBDC while they conducted a national search for a permanent director. Currently, Steve is the Entrepreneurship Director at Pikes Peak Community College and writes a daily blog about small businesses.

Steve is a flaming dyslexic, which has its good points and bad points. Growing up, he remembers undergoing a board of education evaluation. When asked to draw a tree, Steve drew a series of concentric rings. When asked about his drawing, he said the rings were what you see when you cut down the tree and look at the stump. These rings tell the entire life story of the tree. The evaluator told his parents he was not normal. He should be more like the other kids and draw the tree from the side view.

However, rather than conform to the crowd, Steve embraced his out-of-the-box thinking as an asset. The upside of being dyslexic is exceptional spatial awareness and problems solving skills. Dyslexics develop these heightened skills since they are forced from an early age to compensate for things they do not do well.

Being a dyslexic in school prevented Steve from becoming a good reader. Even today, spelling and grammar are not his strong suits. Academically, Steve struggled in traditional schools. When he graduated from high school, he knew that a traditional classroom education was not for him so he joined the United States Coast Guard to learn a trade. Graduating near the top of his class in tech school, Steve realized that he learned by doing.

Steve tends to be an overly logical person. He likes to explore, document, and measure nearly every aspect of a project to find out what works and what does not. He has a propensity to focus on understanding why things are the way they are rather than how to duplicate what others have already done. Once Steve obtains a reasonable level of mastery in a specific subject area, he internalizes the knowledge and moves on to his next area of interest.

Everything of substance Steve knows about small business initially began by him reading books, listening to audiobooks, or watching others. He internalizes the salient points, then rolls up his sleeves and puts them into practice in his own business. Once Steve perfects a lesson, he makes it a point to document it and then share it with others. He calls these "Sea Stories," leveraging his old Coast Guard days. In addition to sharing his knowledge, this practice serves to further solidify his learning in his own mind while continuing to grow his knowledge base. In this way, Steve has codified over more than a decade's worth of his small business knowledge in the various books he has written.

This process has served Steve pretty well. By the time he was 42 years old, Steve had reached the point where he no longer needed to work for money. Passing this income milestone has not only allowed him the luxury to spend even more time to ponder and digest life's lessons, but also the freedom to tell it like it is without the fear of losing his job. He proudly wears jeans nearly every day. He also sports facial hair to remind himself and others that being a nonconformist and not subscribing to traditional viewpoints has its merits for entrepreneurs.

Steve constantly reads and listens to non-fiction audiobooks about politics or business related topics. He consumes current events from a huge basket of news sources every day so he can relate their messages in new and innovative ways. After internalizing a message and testing new theories, he shares his new-found wisdom with people willing to listen.

Since 2003, Steve has mentored and counseled thousands of fledgling entrepreneurs through his volunteer efforts with SCORE and SBDC. He has volunteered his expertise to help organizations like ARC, a program which helps individuals with developmental disabilities.

As cliché as it may sound, Steve is at the point in his life where it is all about using his skills and knowledge to help others to succeed. Steve never expects anything in return, but simply enjoys the appreciation he receives from the people he has helped and lives vicariously through their success. For Steve, sharing his knowledge is akin to the feeling a billionaire might have handing out $100 bills to random strangers on the street. He knows that by sharing some of the wisdom he has accumulated with clients, he can often make a positive difference in their lives. Steve is not particularly religious so helping entrepreneurs is his way of giving back and making a significant impact on the world around him.

Table of Contents

The Elements of An Offer

Every entrepreneur and salesperson should understand the elements of an offer. Every person contemplating a purchase of any kind effectively looks for answers to four key questions when they encounter a salesperson.

1. What is it you are selling?
2. How much it will cost me?
3. What is in it for me?
4. Why should I buy from you?

Therefore, whenever you are selling a product, a service, or just trying to sell someone on a new idea, you would be best served to make sure you answer these four key elements in your sales presentation.

Does your offer include all four elements a customer needs to make a buying decision?

Improve Sales-Target: Customer vs. Consumer

The consumer of a product or service may be different from the customer. A "Customer" is someone that pays for goods or services, while a "Consumer" is someone that uses goods or services.

Often the terms are used interchangeably, but each requires a different message during the sales process. Consider a business that provides piano lessons. If asked what they do, most people in that business would say "I teach my client to play the piano". Often, however, the person receiving the lessons is a child. In the child's case the teacher is correct; they are teaching the child to play music.

The message to the consumer might involve how popular they might be or how proud their parents might be if they could play the piano well. However, while the child is the consumer, they are not the customer.

Mom and dad are the customers. While mom and dad might want their child to learn to play the piano, a savvy salesperson would understand that in addition to providing piano lessons to the child, they might also indicate that they provide a day-care of sorts, allowing mom and/or dad to take care of things while the lessons are being conducted. The savvy businessperson might also tell parents that right brain activities can improve academic scores, which might lead to college scholarship opportunities.

Effectively, the message changes the "What's in it for me" part of the sales pitch to target the customer.

Does the focus of your sales pitch change depending on whether you are talking to the consumer or the customer?

The Power of Free Samples

I was walking through Sam's Club the other day with a shopping list. Nowhere on my list was cheese or ham patties. But as I walked up and down the aisles grazing on samples, I ended up with cheese and ham patties my cart.

There is no way I would have looked at either of these products and said "why not, let's give it a try". Free is free so I tried it and liked it. Now these products are on my shopping list the next time I get back to Sam's Club.

Would you ever buy an expensive bottle of wine without sampling the vintage first? Offering free samples is a powerful way to get new customers for your product or service.

How can you offer a free sample to gain a new customer?

What is the Balance of Your Network Deposits Account?

The best salesman I ever knew was a master of network deposits. He was an insurance salesman and every six months or so he would invite me to lunch. When I showed up he was never alone. He always had someone that provided some type of business service, such as a bookkeeper, CPA, banker, or lawyer. For the first fifteen minutes he would go about introducing me and stroking my ego, telling this new person how great I was.

What he was doing was making network deposits into my account. After this wonderful introduction I felt somewhat indebted to him for saying so many nice things about me. When the meeting was over, the weight of his network deposits created a desire in me to somehow repay his kindness. I often brought up the subject of my insurance coverage and frequently increased my policy limits or added another type of coverage without him even asking me for more of my business.

Furthermore, feeling a bit smug, I frequently replaced an incumbent team member with the services of the guest he brought to lunch, thereby creating another network deposit back to my insurance guy for providing me with the introduction.

One Saturday I had a gardening question and called several

garden shops for advice. One shop spent over twenty minutes providing me with free technical information and even swapping pictures via cell phone to help me understand and take the proper steps to resolve my issues. They never once asked me to buy a product from them. Even though they are over twenty miles away and there are a dozen similar shops much closer, I would never think about getting my supplies from any other garden shop.

The concept of network deposits is simply making network deposits in another's network account in the the form of introductions, connections, advice or even simple flattery, with no direct expectation of any reciprocal action on the other party's part. The sheer weight of a series of one-way network deposits creates a desire in the receiving person to pay the network deposit back or forward.

How can you use the concept of network deposits to improve your sales?

How to Make Money in a Declining Market Space

All businessmen and businesswomen recognize that when the economy is growing customers buy and businesses expand, creating new sales opportunities. However, sales opportunities exist in declining markets, too.

When consumers cut back they look for savings. How can you repackage or reprice your offerings to provide savings to your consumer? Perhaps you can offer an all-you-can-eat plan, add volume discounts, or create a "buy four get one free" offer.

When companies or governments cut back they consolidate and outsource non-key functions. Can your service offerings extend to a new customer base looking to outsource a function previously performed in-house?

Moreover, a bad economy kills off poorly managed or over-extended businesses.

Are any of your competitors about to go under and release their customers into the market?

Influencing Styles

We all have a predominant influencing style when working with others. However, we often need to change our influencing style based on various conditions. At their core there are styles that have a kind of push energy and others that employ more of a pull type energy.

Influencing styles with a push energy involve Persuading or Asserting your position, while Bridging and Attraction are examples of more of a pull energy.

The first influencing style is **Persuading**. When we persuade we either propose ideas, make suggestions, provide recommendations, or we apply reasoning by providing facts or logic in support or in opposition to a position. When it comes to persuading we must either have exclusive information or be working with another party that respects our competence.

The next influencing style is **Asserting**. When we assert our influence we state our expectations through demands, imposing standards, or providing a prescription, or we may use incentives or pressure to control others. When it comes to asserting we must have positional power and must be happy with compliance, more so than the other party's commitment.

The next influencing style is **Bridging**. When we bridge we involve the other party through solicitation and encouraging participation, or we employ listening skills and paraphrase and summarize the other position. Perhaps we could disclose mistakes, make ourselves vulnerable, and ask for help. Bridging is effective when there are emotions involved and the other person is just as committed to the outcome as you are.

The last influencing style is **Attracting**. When we attract we either find common ground by highlighting our common values and beliefs, or we can employ "visioning", where we use a metaphor or analogy to paint a picture of our desired outcome. When it comes to attracting you must share common values and have the other person's trust.

Not all influencing styles work in every situation. Savvy entrepreneurs will change their influencing style based on different situations.

How adept are you at understanding and changing your influencing behaviors based on different situations?

How to Use CPA to Fire Loser Customers

The acronym CPA in this case stands for Customer Profitability Analysis. Many businesses have customers who take advantage of them, to the detriment of other good customers.

To understand CPA the entrepreneur needs to understand the concepts of direct and indirect expenses. Direct expenses equate to the cost of goods sold (COGS) and any labor directly billable to the customer. Indirect expenses are all the expenses that occur and are not billable directly to the customer, such as rent, loan payments, and overhead labor.

Good customers cover all direct costs, their share of indirect costs, plus they contribute to the company's profits.

Laggard customers cover all direct costs, plus contribute at least in some part to their share of indirect costs.

Loser customers don't even cover their direct cost. The best entrepreneurs are quick to fire their loser customers so they go to their competitors.

Laggard customers need to be examined to see if they can be converted to good customers. Even if you can't convert a laggard customer to a good customer you may want to keep them around if you have any extra capacity, as they at least pay a portion of your indirect costs.

Finally, good customers should demand the bulk of your attention to make sure they remain your customers.

Do you have loser customers who deserve to be fired?

Are they taking up your precious resources at the expense of your good customers?

Do you have a plan to turn your laggard customers into good customers?

There's No Such Thing as a Cold Call

If you are a savvy entrepreneur, you don't go into anything cold. With the Internet and a plethora of other resources, you can warm up any call quickly, and not waste your time or your potential client's.

Doing your homework first is one of the best ways to get an advantage over your competition. If you are reaching out to a business you need to understand more about the people in the company you will be speaking to.

Before I call on a company I search the company's web page to get a sense of the business. Often the web page will list the President and other key employees you may encounter.

You can also go to www.wysk.com to get a company profile, information on the officers and directors, as well as other valuable data.

I then do a Google search on the business's principles. Often you will get Facebook, LinkedIn and other social media sites for the people, as well as other useful information to better understand what makes them tick.

Finally, many libraries subscribe to a tool called Reference USA. Reference USA contains a consumers/lifestyle database. By entering the name of a person you can learn about their interests based on their buying history.

In the end there is no such thing as a cold call.

What tools do you use to know more about your customers?

9 Things Every Customer Wants

Do you know what your customer wants? I believe that pretty much every customer wants the same nine things, although they may look slightly different depending upon the industry. They want:

1. More sales
2. Greater productivity
3. More profits
4. A better image
5. More customers
6. Loyal customers
7. Better morale
8. No hassles
9. More free time

If you can satisfy one or all of your customers' wants better than the other guy, you have a recipe for success.

Are you satisfying your customers' wants?

Complex Sales

Business to Consumer (B2C) sales are generally what I call simple sales, where the customer or buyer is also the consumer of the product or service. This means that one person is both the decision maker and the consumer. Show that person the value and they will buy.

Business to Business (B2B) sales, when they involve a larger company, are what I consider complex sales. Complex sales involve at least three distinctly different people in a company, each of whom have different requirements.

First there is **the money guy**, who controls the purse strings. The money guy is interested in Return On Investment (ROI) and profits.

Then, there is **the purchasing department guy**, who acts as the gatekeeper and whose job it is keep you out. Purchasing is interested in the amount of insurance or bonding you have and your past performance.

Finally, there is **the technical guy**, or the person who needs your product or service. The technical guy is interested in how your product or service can solve his problems.

Complex sales require that you prepare presentations to address the needs of all three parties.

Do your complex sales presentations serve the informational needs of all parties?

Tips to Make Successful Sales Calls

Often sales to small to midsize companies require that you make contact with the President or CEO, who is the final decision maker.

The first barrier to speaking with the decision maker is getting past the receptionist or secretary. When calling on a new potential customer it is always good to know who you want to talk to. Asking to speak to the "President" or "CEO" means you have not done your research on the prospect, and will nearly always get you to his/her voice-mail as a polite brush off.

Using the decision maker's name when speaking to the gatekeeper gives you slightly better odds of getting to speak to a real person.

Previously, we looked at research tools to warm up cold calls, but absent any real data to work with, I find it is best to ask to speak to someone in sales. Access to a salesperson is often an open gate, and it is my experience that salespeople are often the most chatty employees of the company. They will often tell you who the decision makers are.

If you begin to get the run around and it is still unclear who will be making the decision, ask "How will the decision to buy my (product or service) be made?" If they don't provide the name of the decision maker, follow up with the question "Then what?" until you get the name of the final decision maker.

When you finally get to the decision maker and s/he makes a pricing objection, I find the following statement to help: "Price or profit, which would you rather have? Price lasts for a moment, profit lasts for a lifetime."

What processes are you using to get to the decision maker?

How to Canvass a Neighborhood

When you have a company that sells Business to Consumer (B2C), canvassing a neighborhood in the early stages of the business when you have more time then money can often be an effective way to gain customers.

When ringing a stranger's doorbell, it is best to start out with a few non-business questions/statements to build rapport. These can be basic openers like "Can you believe this weather" or "What a lovely house you have, how long have you lived here?" Or there's always my favorite, "What a beautiful dog, is he friendly?" Everyone loves a dog lover.

Once you have used a few statements/questions to build a rapport, it is time to deliver the pitch or presentation. People take in 69% more information using their eyes than their ears. To make your presentation or pitch more efficient, use photos, drawings, or a product demo.

Then ask for the sale and be prepared to overcome any objections. Canvassing can be very time consuming, so it is a good idea to qualify your prospect early in the process.

I also find it helpful to dress like the prospect. When I ask permission to hunt a new property I try to dress like a farmer or rancher to make my prospects feel more at ease.

In the early stages of one of my businesses my partner and I were making door to door calls on several rafting companies in Colorado. We tried to look professional and were dressed in dark suits. Often we would enter our target establishment only to find the place empty.

On one call we could see someone beside the building, but as we drove up they disappeared behind the building. Just like many of the other sites, when we walked in the door no one was there to greet us. Needing to make a sale, we walked around behind the building. We discovered our prospect was purposely hiding, thinking that we were from the IRS or some other government agency. Either way, the bearers of bad news. We went to the nearest Wal-Mart, bought a change of clothes, and had much better luck.

When you are talking to a new prospect, observe their body language for signals that you need to adjust your message.

- Look at their **eyes**. If they are looking around you might be losing their interest.
- Look at their **mouth**. If they are not smiling you may be too serious. Making them laugh is always a good sales tactic.
- Also look at their **hands**. If the prospect is fidgeting or wringing their hands, it means they are bored.
- Finally, look at their **arms**. If they are crossed, the prospect is not receptive to your message.

Making unsolicited face to face calls, although time consuming, costs the entrepreneur very little in terms of money and may help a new business to make its first few sales.

Would canvassing a neighborhood, especially one where you have made a previous sale, be worth your time and effort?

Being Funny Pays Dividends in Sales

Ever wonder what makes a good salesperson? While there are many attributes that make a good salesperson, being able to make the customer laugh is one of the most important.

Humor creates a positive emotional connection between the salesperson and the customer. It breaks down some of the initial objection barriers while directing the customer's energy toward the salesperson and his message.

By relaxing the customer, they become more receptive to your message. Poking fun at yourself, your family, or career generally are the best forms of humor.

I have a young dog that often vies for my attention when I'm on the phone. By laughing and joking a bit about the challenges of owning a puppy, which the customer can surely hear in the background, is a great way for me to establish that bond with a potential customer.

Sharing stories about a dumb thing you did or about the process of getting old are good ways to poke fun at yourself and opens the door for improved sales.

Do you use humor when making a sales call?

That Makes Five Senses

We experience life through our five senses. Each of these senses are connected through our unconscious mind to various emotions. When a message touches more than one sense it has multiplying effect to create a stronger memory or help in our recall. Therefore, when selling your product or service, try to incorporate as many senses into your message as possible.

Here is a sales presentation that links to all five senses. Imagine you are a car salesman.

- **SIGHT** – As you walk up to a prospective customer eying one of your cars, you might begin by saying "I really love this model, doesn't she look great?" or pointing out some of the external features of the car.
- **TOUCH** – Then you might ask the prospect to take a seat behind the wheel and encourage him to feel the richness of the leather seats, the way the steering wheel and shifter feel in his hands, or how the air conditioner cools the car quickly on a hot day.
- **SOUND** – Next you might ask the prospect to start the engine so he can hear the power of the engine, or to turn up the radio to hear the awesome sound system, or even close the doors to hear how quiet it is.
- **SMELL** – Perhaps you might then encourage him to take in that new car smell or offer his wife a free

rose if he takes it for a test drive.

- **TASTE** – You might end your presentation by pointing to the cup holder and saying "Imagine driving to work tomorrow with a cup of pumpkin spice latte from Starbucks, not too hot and not too cold," or how nice it will be to take your family out for ice cream in your new car after dinner tonight.

Sometimes your product or service may not lend itself well to a particular sense, such as the sense of taste in our car example. In some cases it may not be important to address all five senses. But as in our example, the pleasurable taste in your prospect's mouth can be linked to a sensory experience he can have with the product of service beyond a literal use of sense. "Can you smell that? It's the money train if you make this investment".

How many senses do you incorporate into your sales presentations?

Two Ears and One Mouth

In Dale Carnegie's book "*How to Win Friends and Influence People*" I first first heard that god gave us two ears and only one mouth to remind us to listen twice as much as we speak.

New salespeople like to jump right in and tell the prospective customer all about a product or service. However, a good salesman lets the customer do most of the talking.

Here are a few question starters to get your prospect talking. "I'm with ABC company where {tag line here}. Do you mind if I ask you a few questions to see if you are a good fit for our {product or service}?

- What do you look for...
- What have you found...
- What has been your experience...
- How do you determine...
- What is the deciding factor...
- What makes/made you choose...
- What do you like about...
- What would you change...
- What do your competitors do about...
- How do your customers react to...

Letting your prospective customer become more involved

in the discussion will provide you all the triggers you will need to make an effective close.

Do you let your customer do most of the talking?

Feature & Benefits

Business to Consumer (B2C) customers often have a "Want" they need filled, but Business to Business (B2B) customers often have a "Need" for your product or service, and are more versed in the potential benefits you can provide.

Therefore, when selling to B2B customers, your sales presentation may only involve pointing out your features and stressing your bottom line benefits. However, for B2C customers, "features tell but benefits sell".

When you are ready to put together a B2C sales pitch I find it helpful to list all the features that your product or service provides. Then, next to each feature answer the question of why that feature was added in the first place. Take each "why" answer and connect it to the prospect's wants from your product and service.

Finally, try to link each answer to an emotion or one or more of the five senses as described earlier in this book.

Does your sales message stress more benefits or features of your product, and is it right for your audience?

Can Your Business Benefit from Priming?

Ever go to a high school dance where the dance floor was empty because nobody wanted to be the first one to dance? Finally one brave couple strolls out, perhaps encouraged to do so by a chaperone or staff member, and before you know it the dance floor is full. You just witnessed "Priming".

Casinos often employ what are know as "Proposition" or "Shill" players who are compensated by the casino to help prime poker tables. Without Proposition or Shill players, gamblers would walk into a casino, look around and walk back out the door. However, the presence of casino-employed players at a table means new players don't have to wait around to start playing, which translates to more revenue for the casino.

I give a lot of presentations for SCORE and the SBDC, and even though I encourage questions from my audience there is often a long time before someone musters the courage to raise the first question. Sometimes I encourage a co-presenter to ask the first question to prime the system. Often once that first question is out of the way the questions keep coming as the flood gates open.

How can your business take advantage of priming?

How to Win a Customer for Life

My wife frequents a bakery that uses punch cards as a loyalty reward for its customers. After you accumulate five punches you get a ten percent discount on your order when you redeem a completed card.

Recently she was at the bakery. When she was ready to check out with a larger order than usual, the cashier leaned over and whispered to my wife that she would double punch her card. My wife was so thrilled that she called several friends just to speak about her unexpected experience. When I spoke to her that evening and she recounted the experience to me I asked her how she felt about the store given the double stamp incident. She said that this random act has made her a customer of that store for life.

Such a simple thing that was so unexpected created such goodwill that not only did my wife share the positive experience, but in her own words is a customer for life.

What simple act of unexpected kindness can you do for your customer to create this level of delight?

Gamification to Build Customer Loyalty and Generate Buzz

Gamification can be a valuable tool to build relationships with your customers.

Many years ago a company claimed to have hidden a case of its whiskey deep in the mountains of Sasquatch country in Oregon. Every few days the company revealed another clue to the treasure map to help someone find the goods. The clues and the potential location of the case of booze were the topic of many conversations, which helped to build the brand.

Another good example of gamification comes from a small specialty beer producer that used picture puzzles. Under each cap was a series of simple pictures and letters that when spoken together created a common phrase. I can remember being pretty much done drinking but wanting to open just one more beer to see if I could solve the puzzle.

Then there are challenges. One bar in my area serves 105 different beers, and issued a passport to its patrons. If you manage to get all the beers stamped on your passport your name is added to their wall of honor.

Lest I leave you with the impression that gamification must involve alcohol, there is always the example of the golden ticket used in the Willy Wonka movie or the ever-popular McDonald's Monopoly game.

Gamification can create not only buzz about your product or service but can also become an effective tool to improve revenues.

How can you use gamification to improve sales in your company?

Have You Seen Your Customer's Ride?

What you drive says a lot about who you are and what you value. I often find it very useful to meet a new person at a location that requires them to drive there, such as a Starbucks. I try to arrive early and get a seat where I can observe the person drive up.

If they drive up in a status car like a Cadillac I know that how others perceive them is very valuable to them, if they drive up in a pickup truck they are likely an outdoorsy person, and if they're on a motorcycle they are a bit rebellious.

While not 100% accurate it serves as a good starting point and I make sure to use that knowledge when building rapport or attempting to influence them later.

In addition to the vehicle itself I look for bumper or window stickers that can provide additional valuable insight as well.

A political sticker such as an Obama sticker reveals their political views and all that comes with that.

Window stickers of turtles or stick figures that represent the family unit can give you clues to the number and genders of kids as well as pets that make up their family.

Jesus or evolution fish tell of their views of creation, and guns or NRA decals give insight into hobbies or how they value the constitution. And the list goes on.

What a person drives and how they personalize it can tell you more in ten seconds than an hour of dialog would provide.

Do you employ tactics to see what a prospect drives so you can adjust your messaging?

Primacy and Recency

Many years ago at a seminar I was presented with a list of about fifteen random words. After the list was presented we were all asked to recall all the words we could remember. Lo and behold, a pattern emerged.

The words at the beginning of the list and the words at the end of the list were most commonly recalled by the seminar participants, while the words in the middle were missed. Also, any words that were unusual among the list, such as a verb in a list of nouns, were also recalled.

The exercise demonstrated what is know as primacy and recency. An understanding of these concepts can help you become a better marketer.

At the beginning of a list our minds are clear, and we make a effort to associate the first few words so we might have better recall. However, as the list continues our minds became overwhelmed, and we fail to make the associations needed to aid memory before the next word is presented. As the list concludes the last few words remain in our short term memory and are more easily retrieved.

Our innate ability as humans to remember the beginning of a conversation is know as primacy, and our ability to recall more recent items is known as recency.

Teaching theory employs this understanding of the human

brain by making sure that the information we most want recalled will occur at the beginning and at the end of the lesson, barring any surprises in the middle. Good marketers also use primacy and recency in their messaging to make sure that potential customers will be be able to recall the most important elements of their message.

Do you use the concept of primacy and recency to make sure your customers remember the message you want them to walk away with?

Customer On A Line

I'm a fly fisherman, and anyone familiar with the sport understands that to land a fish using a fly rod requires a lot of skills. I think I like fly fishing because it is cerebral and has so much in common with B2B sales.

In fly fishing you have to understand in great detail the species you are fishing for. You have to know what they eat and where they hang out, and combine that knowledge with what is going on in their environment, such as water temperature and water flow rates.

In sales you also have to learn about your prospect in great detail. You need to know what is the measure of their business success and what niche they occupy in their industry, and combine this knowledge with external factors like the company's value proposition as compared to their competition and economic factors.

Armed with a game plan, the fly fisherman must select the right fly to attract the attention of the fish. Then he must present it in so delicate a way that he will not spook the fish and make him willfully leave when he is and come to the fly.

In sales you must provide the prospect with enough enticing details about your offer to get him to leave his comfort zone and rise to your offer.

Once the fish takes the fly, the fisherman must know the exact moment to set the hook. He must not be too rough, or he risks breaking the delicate line. He then needs to gently reel the fish in, trying to avoid snags that will allow the fish to get away.

In sales the salesperson must know the exact moment to close the deal and stop talking. He must then manage the process, keeping the pressure on and avoiding snags, until the goods or services are delivered and money is exchanged.

In the end the image of a customer on a fishing line is a powerful image. You can pull him in, but you can't push him to buy.

How do you fish for new customers?

Be Memorable

It was 10:00 pm on April 18th 1775. Two riders left Boston, Massachusetts, to ride out to Lexington and Concord to alert the militia that the British troops were on their way to capture Samuel Adams and John Hancock. Who were these two midnight riders?

My guess is you came up with Paul Revere as one of the riders, but unless you are a history buff you likely don't remember the other rider: William Dawes.

Why do you suppose we remember Paul Revere and don't remember William Dawes? The answer is pretty simple. Paul Revere was a well-known silversmith, while William Dawes was an obscure tanner.

When Paul knocked on a door and said "The British are coming" the homeowners recognized Paul and remembered the messenger. When William knocked on a door and said "The British are coming," well, let's just say they remembered "a guy".

Henry Wadsworth Longfellow later wrote a poem called Paul Revere's Ride. While inaccurate, it solidified Paul's role in history and we all forgot about Mr. Dawes. Paul had hundreds of network connections, and as such was related to the story in ways that William, with far fewer connections, could not be.

So having lots of network connections gets you recognized for your deeds, while having few makes you forgettable.

What are you doing to increase your network connections and be more memorable?

The Drug Dealer's Mindset

As a business coach, one of the single most common issues I see with new entrepreneurs is their lack of understanding of gross profit, gross margin, and the impact of operating expenses. Their focus is almost always exclusively on the revenue gained from sales. I often refer to this as the "drug dealer's mindset."

Petty street level drug dealers are often fronted a bunch of product they are expected to sell for the distributor. As they sell their product, they are left with a fist full of cash, making the drug dealer feel rich and leading them to believe that being a drug dealer is great gig. Unfortunately, what the drug dealer has in his hands is called revenue.

Revenue is the result of sales and is not what makes you rich. A business needs to subtract their cost of goods sold (COGS) from their revenue to equal their gross profit.

Gross profit is what is used to pay operating expenses, including wages. The ratio of gross profit to revenue is known as gross margin. Gross margin is a much more important measurement of a business's health than revenue.

The drug dealer sees the cash generated from his sales, but forgets that the cash is not his. From that cash, he still owes the distributor the cost for the product he was initially fronted or he risks "getting fitted for a pair of cement overshoes," as my dad would say.

What the drug dealer is left with after paying his distributor is gross profit. Gross profit is what he can use to cover any expenses and pay himself for his efforts.

According to a study by the National Bureau of Economic Research, the typical petty drug dealer's average wage is only $6.00-11.00 per hour and many earn far less.

Many books on small business say that businesses live and die based on making sales. However, this is very misleading statement. Small businesses live and die based on their gross profit not from sales. After all, I can always make sales if I sell my product or service for less than my actual cost.

Even big businesses struggle with this distinction. My business was acquired by a publicly held company during the dot-com era for our revenue alone. It was not bought for our gross profits, gross margins, or even the free cash we could provide. In fact, after the acquisition of my business, their business model doubled down on the "revenue only" drug dealer mindset.

After we were acquired we got new customers by agreeing to charge them less than their internal costs. We did this even if it meant our reduced price resulted in a tiny gross margin that would come no where close to covering even a small fraction of our operating expenses resulting in us losing money. We only offered this reduced price if the customers agreed to outsource their entire departments work to our company.

Since we were essentially giving away our services in the name of growing sales, it was no surprise that the division I managed grew from eight to thirty two million dollars in sales in only eighteen months.

Successful entrepreneurs know that it is not revenue or sales that count, but the gross margin you can produce from your sales. Without a healthy gross margin, your sales will not produce enough gross profit to cover your operating expenses and return a profit to the owners.

Do you suffer from the drug dealer's mindset and think only about growing sales or are your focused on how much gross margin your sales will produce?

The Secret to Better Sales

Do you constantly search for techniques, tricks, and gimmicks to sell your product or service to your customers? If you are looking for techniques, tricks, and gimmicks, it will most likely not help because people hate to be sold something. However, they do love to buy.

While it may seem like simple wordsmithing, the conceptual difference is related to the direction of the energy. Selling is pushing while buying is pulling. If you take the time to ask your customers why they buy, you will discover that most of the answers have to do with you.

These answers could include:
- they like you
- have confidence in you
- believe you
- trust you
- and perceive that you are actually trying to help them

Other answers you might hear are:
- they understand what they are buying
- are able to perceive the value of your product/service
- or feel that your price is fair.

The real lesson for someone wanting to be a better sales

person really boils down to establishing a positive relationship with your prospect.

At the beginning of any great sales process is the establishment of the need and desire in the customer for your product or service. I like to think about it as creating gravity for your product or service.

Gravity can be established through either creating fear or greed in the prospect. Our society preys on the fear factor which makes up about 50% of all ads. These ads include messages such as "Our tires are designed to grip the road in the rain so you don't hit that kid on the bike" or "Make your home safe with our security system." You can always count on the media to fan the flames of fear which is why fear is a powerful tool in creating gravity for your product or service.

The other half of marketing appeals to the prospects of greed or vanity. For example, Cadillac's "Work Hard. Be Lucky" slogan and American Express's "Membership has it privileges" slogan both play upon the appeal of greed and vanity.

Once the prospect is under the gravitational influence of your product or services, the final sale is a matter of building a positive relationship with the prospect and being there to answer questions. Once gravitational pull and a positive relation are established, clients will generally do the rest.

Do you have a specific plan to build report with prospective clients?

Stories to Create a Great First Impression

There is a lot of information about the personal side of making a good first impression, such as how to dress, a firm handshake, and so on. However, I'd like to focus on what makes the encounter both memorable and shareable with others.

Everyone loves a story, especially ones that invoke emotions in the listener. Moreover, the human brain likes to link new information to existing information. Rather than leave that process to the other party, help them make the associations you want. A good first impression starts with a visual story, something that the customer can see in his mind's eye and relate to.

The best visual stories tie into four emotional hots spots or trigger points that stimulate the Limbic system of the brain, causing us to involuntary interrupt our preoccupation with something else and pay greater attention to your message.

1.
1. The first emotional trigger point involves **money**, either making it or losing it. We are all motivated to engage in stories that deal with money in some way.
2. The next emotional trigger involves a story that deals with some sort of **self-preservation or security**. We are hardwired to focus on issues of safety whether they concern us physically or financially.
3. The third trigger involves the idea of some sort of

recognition. Our self-talk thrives on ways to achieve some sort of positive recognition.

4. The fourth trigger involves **romance or sex**. Here again we are hardwired to focus on these types of issues for the preservation of the species.

Finally, make sure your stories create the proper images and associations by using similes, metaphors, and analogies to create the proper links in your customer's recall. Some examples include: "...our backhoe's bucket looks like and operates like the head and neck of dinosaur" and "our solar company turns sunshine into money." The visual imagery of your story will standout in your customer's mind and make you more memorable, often leading them to share your story with others.

Do you use stories to make a good first impression?

Cold Calls

Recently, I had a client asked me some questions regarding cold calling techniques. Specifically, he said that he had conducted some market research and came upon a list of people he felt could really benefit from his product and services. He wanted to reach out to them, but was not sure about the best way to set up a face to face meeting since the prospect didn't know him from Adam. He didn't want to get off on the wrong foot by soliciting them right out of the gate.

I believe this is a common problem for small business owners that lacks a silver bullet solution. Having made hundreds of cold calls with various results, here is the process that has proven to be the most effective for me to get a face to face interview.

First, I see if the prospect has connections with anyone on my LinkedIn network. I add all of my current and past clients to my LinkedIn network, provided they have a LinkedIn account. I have discovered that many folks on LinkedIn connect with suppliers, vendors, and even competitors. If one of them has a connection with my prospect, I ask them for an introduction.

Absent of a LinkedIn introduction, I generally attempt to reach out to the prospect by phone first rather than just show up. Since I tend to aim high in an organization, I often get stopped by the gatekeeper secretary or administrative assistant. I explain, "I have some research that I'm sure {name here} would find very interesting and I would like to send it to them in a email message." Sometimes the secretary or administrative assistant gives me their own email address instead of my prospect's email. There is no fighting this. If this is the case, I make sure to get their name so I can do some research on the gatekeeper.

I then send them some research that they may find interesting. In my case, I deal with companies who solicit high net worth investors so I have synthesized some research from several different sources to create a three page report about high net worth investors. Most prospects find this report extraordinarily useful.

At the bottom of the report, I have what I call "the secret sauce message." The report frames the problem and provides a solution. However, I always try to leave the reader with a "wow tell me more" message.

After I send the message, I wait a few days to call the prospect and set up a meeting.

If the gatekeeper has not forwarded the message, they may give you a delay tactic. In this situation, I ask, "When is a better time to call back?" Anticipating this delay tactic, I also try to become friends with the gatekeeper by leveraging the research I conducted earlier. I make it clear to the gatekeeper that I'm following up on the report and I'm looking for feedback. Explaining that I'm following up on report to get his feedback often gets me past the gatekeeper.

This strategy of providing something of value and trying to get their feedback on it shows I have their best interest in mind and forces me not to launch into my sales pitch when I get an audience.

How do you get a face to face meeting with a new prospect?

Network Events

Networking events for me are not about selling, but for listening and gathering intelligence. You will be viewed as a great conversationalist at networking events if you resist the urge to sell and get the other person to talk about themselves and their business.

One of the questions I ask nearly all new contacts is "What keeps you up at night?" This is a great way to get the contact to reveal their pain points. It is essential that you understand their problems before you try to pitch them a solution.

After the encounter, I take a few notes either on the back of their business card or on a separate notepad to capture the salient points of our conversation. I not only record the talking points, but I also assign a priority to the contact and any actions I agreed to provide.

I make it a goal to get quality information on about three contacts at every networking event, more if it is an Expo type of event. However, for many people, networking events stop here.

Did you know that after a networking event only about 20% of the people follow up on the contacts they made? It perplexes me why 80% of the people even attend these events if they do nothing with the information they gathered. Perhaps the 80% were more interested in selling than gathering information. Maybe they are hoping that their contact will be so impressed by their selling skills that they will contact them after the event. Therefore, you can instantly be in the top 20% simply by following up with the contacts you made.

When you get back to your office, do not resume business as usual. Consider the first few hours back at the office as part of the networking event. Break out the business cards and send each contact you made an email message. The content of the email should not be "glad we had a chance to meet." Instead, do an online search for an article or website that addresses a possible solution to their problems and include this reference in the email.

Give it a day or two and then search for them on LinkedIn. Send them a connection request. After contacting them three times (meeting, email, and LinkedIn), you will certainly be a memorable contact.

How do you handle networking events?

16 Principles to Influence a Sale

Have you ever wanted something so badly that you would do anything to get it? That feeling does not happen over night; a sales process created that yearning inside you. In their book, "Rainmaking Conversations," Mike Schultz and John Doerr list 16 ways to make your customers reach that level of desire.

1. **Attention** – People are preoccupied and the first step in any sales process is to get their attention. Read my blog post called "Stories to Create a Great First Impression" to learn how to use the four emotional appeals to snap a person out of their preoccupation and focus on you.

2. **Curiosity** – Once you get the prospect's attention, you must make them curious enough to want to know more. I recommend you develop a WOW statement to pique their curiosity. The WOW statement comes from the premise that after you deliver your statement, the other party has to respond with "Wow, tell me more." Read the blog post "How to Create a WOW Statement" for more information on WOW statements.

3. **Desire** – Desire is the gap between where your prospect is now and where they want to be. This is where a discussion of their return on investment (ROI) comes into play so the customer can see what is in it for him. To intensify their desire, a good salesman knows that he may have to fan the flames

of dissatisfaction with the present situation and point out the possibilities your product or service will provide.

4. **Envy** – Envy is the desire supercharger. Envy is when the customer wants something and wants it more when he sees that others have it. He feels an intense desire to obtain it out of the fear that without it the gap between him and others will widen. It will continue to eat away at him day and night until he gets it.

5. **Emotional** Journey – As we pointed out in "Stories to Create a Great First Impression," a goods salesman is a storyteller who can trigger deep seated emotions and images in the other person. You need to be able to deliver a story that will create a lasting image and emotion in your prospect. As an animal lover, I am deeply moved by animal cruelty commercials. These commercials exemplifies how to create an emotional journey for your audience.

6. **Belief** – The customer can't remain skeptical on whether or not your product or service will work for them. They have to believe your product or service can and will do what you say it can. They must believe in you. To reinforce this, you must show them that you consistently do what you say you will do and that your brand has a history of success. One way to accomplish this is to provide demonstrations so your customers can see that your product does what you say it will. Another way is to provide

testimonials from others as proof of the quality of your services.

7. **Justification** – People make decisions on emotion and justify them with logic. Even if your solution makes logical sense, it needs to be tied to an emotion. The promise of their ROI is the reason the customer listens you. It is not the ROI of making more money that will get them to buy; it is the image of how much happier they will be with more money that is the emotional key.

8. **Trust** – The customer must trust you. He must know that you know what you are talking about, have a history of reliability, and are not a risky bet that will come back to bite him. Finally he must know that you will not take advantage of him if it suits you.

9. **Stepping Stones** – People are more interested in things they are familiar with. A good salesman takes the customer from something he is familiar with to the solution the salesman wants the customer to embrace by going through a series of steps. Sometimes this process is called the Domino Strategy. In essence, you are trying to shorten the customer's leap of faith by peeling away the layers of an onion one by one so he can make the journey to the solution.

10. **Ownership** – Until the customer takes ownership of the solution, your influence is limited. A customer that says "OK, let's try it" is not yet on board. The customer must want to own the solution. Without

ownership, the customer will not devote themselves to the solution and others may talk him out of it.

11. **Involvement** – When the customer has a hand in the solution, he is more likely to be a passionate advocate. Make your customers part of the solution. Ask them their opinion and have them help in coming up with answers.

12. **Desire for Inclusion** – People may say that they are not influenced by the actions of others, but they are. When a person's perspective is not shared by most others, they are more likely to accept the perspective of others. They assume that the other people must know something they don't. The use of social proofs in the forms of testimonials and statistics, like "25% of Fortune 500 companies use our product," help stroke the customer's desire for inclusion.

13. **Scarcity** – "Buy it now! Only 2 left!" is a phrase we often hear. Scarcity is the most commonly employed persuasion technique. People value things that are rare even if that rarity is man made. The Debeer's company artificially kept diamond prices high by controlling supply. Moreover, people fear loss more than gains

14. **Likeability** – When it comes to being liked, we are talking about the customer having an affinity towards you. However, your desire to be liked by the customer should not be overshadowed by the need to make the sale. People pay attention, listen, and buy from people they like.

15. **Indifference** – Desperation is not a good influencing strategy. You need to be OK with not making the deal. Be happy with walking away if the situation warrants.
16. **Commitment** – When someone makes a public commitment, they are much more likely to keep them. I made a public announcement that I was writing my first book and because the announcement was public, I was more committed to getting it done. Once the customer signs off on the deal, make a public announcement to keep them committed.

Which of these sixteen principles do you use to influence a sale?

What Is in a Name

Hoover Adams was the editor for a small local newspaper in the rural community of Dunn North Carolina. This newspaper was called the <u>Daily Record</u>.

What makes the Daily Record unique is while other newspapers were struggling to maintain readership, the Daily Record led the nation in circulation penetration. In fact, the Daily Record was selling more newspapers to their primary market than there were homes. To be more specific, their penetration rate was 117 percent.

How could a small local paper buck the national trend and actually sell more than one paper per household? The answer lies in the content. Hoover had one clear message for his staff: "Names, Names, Names." The Daily Record only published stories about the people in the local community.

There were no national news and no state level news. There were only stories that had something to do with local citizens whose names were plastered throughout each edition because, as he said, everyone loves to see their name in print.

Businesses can learn a lot from Hoover Adams and the Daily Record. Recognizing a person by including their names wherever and whenever you can will build loyalty. As Dale Carnegie said, "Remember that a person's name is to that person the sweetest and most important sound in any language."

Do you include other people's names in conversations and in print wherever you can?

Sales Acceleration Emails

So, you have a potential customer's email address. How do you get him to take action and accept your offer? You have to appeal to their unique buyer psychology. One size does not fit all when it comes to why customers hesitate to click on the "Buy Now" button. When it comes to making online purchases, there are four main types of buyer psychologies. Using a series of emails, you can appeal to these different types of buyers.

Urgent Email

The goal of the urgent email is to remind the customer that there is a time limit inherent in the offer. Some buyers need that extra push to get them to make a decision now. Urgent emails should highlight the savings that are available only if they act now as well as the benefits involved with this special offer.

FAQ Email

The goal of the FAQ email is to appeal to customers with an analytical and logical mind set. These buyers resist offers based on uncertainty or because they have unanswered questions. FAQ emails should focus on filling in details with a question and answer format. Some common questions your FAQ email needs to address include:

- What do I get in the offer?
- How much does this special offer cost versus regular price?
- What bonuses are included? What kind of guarantee do you offer?

Testimonial Email

The goal of the testimonial email is to appeal to people who respond best to stories from others. Through the narrative, you want to help the potential customer imagine using the product themselves. You want to add fuel to their imagination based on the experience of others. There is no better fuel to rev up a person's imagination than real life experiences from others.

Last Day Email

The goal of the last day email is to appeal to those who procrastinate. Some people are just hardwired to wait until the last possible minute no matter what. The last day email is meant to give this potential customer a little push to get them off the dime. Most people with procrastinating mindsets would say that they wanted your offer when they were first exposed to it. However, their mindset inclines them put off the purchase until later. They intended to follow up, but simply forget and are happy for the reminder.

How do your offers appeal to the four buyer psychologies?